30 DAYS OF
OPTIMAL

ACHIEVING GREATNESS
IN MIND, BODY, AND SOUL

BY: JARED ZIMMERER

Other titles by Jared Zimmerer

Ten Commandments of Lifting Weights:

Recommendations to the Devout Body Builder

Man Up!

Becoming the New Catholic Renaissance Man

Cover Design: Jared Zimmerer

Interior Design: Jared Zimmerer

Printed in the United States of America

First Printing, 2015

ISBN-13: 978-0692611241 (Bohemond Press)

ISBN-10: 069261124X

www.jaredzimmerer.com

THIS BOOK IS DEDICATED TO MY WIFE, JESSICA AND MY CHILDREN, ETHAN, BRUCE, FULTON, ADRIANNA AND LEO, AS WELL AS ANY OTHER CHILDREN WHICH MAY COME.

REQUIREMENTS OF OPTIMAL LIVING

α DESIRES RESULTS OVER COMFORT

α DESIRES A STRONG BODY, A STRONG MIND, AND A STRONG SPIRIT

α DESIRES INTEGRITY, COURAGE, AND HONESTY

α DESIRES WORK ETHIC AND DRIVE TO SUCCEED

α DESIRES KNOWLEDGE OF HUMANITY ON MANY PLANES

α DESIRES AWARENESS OF THE UNSEEN

α DESIRES TO SHAPE ONE'S ENVIRONMENT RATHER THAN BE SHAPED BY IT.

LIST OF APPROVED FOODS

PROTEINS:

Whole Eggs
Fish
Beef
Chicken
Pork

CARBOHYDRATES: *We will not be counting calories over this period of time. The only thing you'll be counting is carb intake*

Brown or White Rice (45 grams per cup)
Oatmeal (27 grams per cup)
Sweet Potatoes (approx. 27 grams per potato)
White Potatoes (approx. 33 grams per potato)

FATS:

Butter
Avocadoes
Hummus
Peanut Butter (Natural)
Olive Oil

RULES ON FRUITS, DAIRY, ALCOHOL, AND VEGETABLES

VEGETABLES

Eat as much as you want!
Try and stick with green veggies but any veggie is better than no veggies.

FRUITS

For the next 30 days, fruits are off limits. They are not bad for you. This thirty days is about discipline and leaning out carbohydrates. Fruits contain cheap carbs. (Avocados are technically a fruit, but come on, don't hold me on that.)

DAIRY

You may eat or drink dairy once a day. This would include cottage cheese, whole milk and Greek yogurt. Buy the flavorless Greek yogurt if you go with that option.

ALCOHOL

Absolutely no alcohol during this time.

PHYSICAL CAVEAT

The workouts in this book are meant for those who are already in decent physical condition. Should you be unable to complete the entire routines my biggest suggestion is to follow the dietary restrictions. However, even those who are not physically able to complete the entire routine, WORK, so that eventually you can. If you don't finish each day, that's fine, but work hard, eat right and do your absolute best. This journey is about improvement, you can only improve if you are willing to put in the sweat and toil.

If you'll notice, the only restriction you will be paying attention to is carbohydrate intake. Don't worry about calories; don't worry about proteins, only worry about carbohydrates. This simplifies the process and makes the challenge doable. Should you be hungry once you've hit your carb intake for the day, proteins and vegetables have absolutely no limit, so eat up!

MENTAL CAVEAT

Some of these daily readings are going to be difficult to understand without a background in some philosophy and theology. However, my challenge to you is to read it anyway. Read it several times if you have to. The whole point is to challenge your intellectual capacity and just like working out you have to stretch your limits. If you don't understand it on the first run, that's perfectly fine. Read it several times throughout the day if you have to. Other readings will motivate and inspire you, I highly recommend the same attention to detail.

SPIRITUAL CAVEAT

The spiritual aspect of this book takes two avenues. Each day provides questions for you to consider during a quiet time of reflection. The main facet of these questions is to ask one of the most important questions you should continually ask yourself, 'who am I?'. Socrates considered this question the most important of all philosophy. The second avenue is within the readings as a few of them contain thoughts about God, nature, beauty and the like all asking our souls to recognize that which is beyond the physical.

DAY 1: MONDAY

5:00 A.M. WAKE UP

30 push-ups
30 sit-ups
30 body squats

TODAY'S WORKOUT: CHEST AND BACK

Bench Press: 3 X 8
Incline Dumbbell Press: 3 X 10
Flat Bench Dumbbell Flyes: 3X 15
Dips: 3 sets to Failure

Wide Grip Pulldowns: 3 X 8
Cable Rows: 3 x 10
Dumbbell Rows: 3 X 15
Chin Ups: 3 sets to Failure

DIET:
Eat under 100 carbs

DAY 1: MONDAY

READING FOR REFLECTION

We must take as a sign of states of character the pleasure or pain that ensues on acts; for the man who abstains from bodily pleasures and delights in this very fact is temperate, while the man who is annoyed at it is self-indulgent, and he who stands his ground against things that are terrible and delights in this or at least is not pained is brave, while the man who is pained is a coward. For moral excellence is concerned with pleasures and pains; it is on account of the pleasure that we do bad things, and on account of the pain that we abstain from noble ones. Hence we ought to have been brought up in a particular way from our very youth, as Plato says, so as both to delight in and to be pained by the things that we ought; for this is the right education.

Again, it is harder to fight with pleasure than with anger, to use Heraclitus' phrase', but both art and virtue are always concerned with what is harder; for even the good is better when it is harder. Therefore for this reason also the whole concern both of virtue and of political science is with pleasures and pains; for the man who uses these well will be good, he who uses them badly bad.   – Aristotle, *Nicomachean Ethics*

DAY 1: MONDAY

SPIRITUAL MEDIATION

(Find a quiet place to reflect. Breathe deeply and calm the mind. Once your heart rate slows, consider the following questions.)

- α How often am I seeking comfort in place of results?

- α What is it in my life that I want to achieve?

- α Where am I currently in feeling fulfillment in my life?

DAY 2: TUESDAY

5:00 A.M. WAKE UP

30 push-ups
30 sit-ups
30 body squats

TODAY'S WORKOUT: CARDIO

Find a time today when you can devote 30
minutes to a brisk walk.

DIET:

Eat under 100 carbohydrates

DAY 2: TUESDAY

READING FOR REFLECTION

Seeing this then, and noting well the faculties which you have, you should say,—"Send now, O God, any trial that Thou wilt; lo, I have means and powers given me by Thee to acquit myself with honour through whatever comes to pass!"— No; but there you sit, trembling for fear certain things should come to pass, and moaning and groaning and lamenting over what does come to pass. And then you upbraid the Gods. Such meanness of spirit can have but one result— impiety.

Yet God has not only given us these faculties by means of which we may bear everything that comes to pass without being crushed or depressed thereby; but like a good King and Father, He has given us this without let or hindrance, placed wholly at our own disposition, without reserving to Himself any power of impediment or restraint.

Yet what faculties and powers you possess for attaining courage and greatness of heart, I can easily show you; what you have for upbraiding and accusation, it is for you to show me!

α   Epictetus, *The Golden Sayings of Epictetus*

DAY 2: TUESDAY

SPIRITUAL MEDIATION

(Find a quiet place to reflect. Breathe deeply and calm the mind. Once your heart rate slows, consider the following questions.)

α What powers and talents have I been given that I am not using?

α What powers and talents am I using well?

α Who in my life might I be willing to share my powers and talents with by helping them in their needs?

DAY 3: WEDNESDAY

5:00 A.M. WAKE UP

30 push-ups
30 sit-ups
30 body squats

TODAY'S WORKOUT: LEGS AND SHOULDERS

Leg Press: 3 X 8
Squat: 3 X 8
Leg Extensions: 3 X 15
Straight-leg Deadlift: 3 X 10

Standing front press: 3 X 8
Lateral dumbbell raises: 3 X 10
Front barbell raises: 3 X 10
Standing upright rows: 3 X 10

DIET:

Eat under 100 carbohydrates

DAY 3: WEDNESDAY

READING FOR REFLECTION

If each year should see one fault rooted out from us, we should go quickly on to perfection. But on the contrary, we often feel that we were better and holier in the beginning of our conversion than after many years of profession. Zeal and progress ought to increase day by day; yet now it seemeth a great thing if one is able to retain some portion of his first ardour. If we would put some slight stress on ourselves at the beginning, then afterwards we should be able to do all things with ease and joy.

It is a hard thing to break through a habit, and a yet harder thing to go contrary to our own will. Yet if thou overcome not slight and easy obstacles, how shalt thou overcome greater ones? Withstand thy will at the beginning, and unlearn an evil habit, lest it lead thee little by little into worse difficulties. Oh, if thou knewest what peace to thyself thy holy life should bring to thyself, and what joy to others, methinketh thou wouldst be more zealous for spiritual profit.

- Thomas à Kempis, *The Imitation of Christ*

DAY 3: WEDNESDAY

SPIRITUAL MEDIATION

(Find a quiet place to reflect. Breathe deeply and calm the mind. Once your heart rate slows, consider the following questions.)

α   What bad habits am I having trouble breaking? What steps am I taking to rid myself of those?

α   What good habits am I continually growing in?

α   How have my bodily habits or lake thereof, such as disciplined eating, affected other areas of my life?

DAY 4: THURSDAY

5:00 A.M. WAKE UP

30 push-ups
30 sit-ups
30 body squats

TODAY'S WORKOUT: CARDIO

30 burpees
100 jumping jacks
20 burpees

DIET:

Eat under 100 carbohydrates

DAY 4: THURSDAY

READING FOR REFLECTION

BEGIN the morning by saying to thyself, I shall meet with the busybody, the ungrateful, arrogant, deceitful, envious, unsocial. All these things happen to them by reason of their ignorance of what is good and evil. But I who have seen the nature of the good that it is beautiful and of the bad that it is ugly, and the nature of him who does wrong, that it is akin to me, not [only] of the same blood or seed, but that it participates in [the same] intelligence and [the same] portion of the divinity, I can neither be injured by any of them, for no one can fix on me what is ugly, nor can I be angry with my kinsman, nor hate him. For we are made for co-operation, like feet, like hands, like eyelids, like the rows of the upper and lower teeth. To act against one another then is contrary to nature; and it is acting against one another to be vexed and to turn away.

- Marcus Aurelius, *The Meditations*

DAY 4: THURSDAY

SPIRITUAL MEDIATION

(Find a quiet place to reflect. Breathe deeply and calm the mind. Once your heart rate slows, consider the following questions.)

α What's my current morning routine look like? In what ways can I improve it?

α Do I prepare my mind each day to deal with difficult situations?

α Which challenges am I facing in my desire to accomplish fulfillment?

DAY 5: FRIDAY

5:00 A.M. WAKE UP

30 push-ups
30 sit-ups
30 body squats

TODAY'S WORKOUT: ARMS

Barbell Bicep Curls: 3 X 8
Dumbbell Incline Curls: 3 X 10
Cable Rope Curls: 3 X 12

Close-grip bench press: 3 X 8
Incline French Press: 3 X 10
Triceps Dips: 3 X 15

Chin-ups: 2 sets to failure

DIET:

Eat under 100 carbohydrates

DAY 5: FRIDAY

READING FOR REFLECTION

Had I the heaven's embroidered cloths,
Enwrought with golden and silver light,
The blue and the dim and the dark cloths
Of night and light and the half-light;
I would spread the cloths under your feet:
But I, being poor, have only my dreams;
I have spread my dreams under your feet;
Tread softly because you tread on my dreams.

- W. B. Yeats, *The Cloths of Heaven*

DAY 5: FRIDAY

SPIRITUAL MEDIATION

(Find a quiet place to reflect. Breathe deeply and calm the mind. Once your heart rate slows, consider the following questions.)

α   We all have dreams. Some to accomplish. Some to change. Still others to keep us driven. What specific steps am I taking to achieve my desires?

α   Who might there be for me to reach out to in order to keep me accountable in my discipline of accomplishing what I want to?

α   Money can only fill a need. Where am I searching for true interior fulfillment?

DAY 6: SATURDAY

5:00 A.M. WAKE UP

40 push-ups
40 sit-ups
40 body squats

TODAY'S WORKOUT: CARDIO

Find a time today when you can devote 30
minutes to a brisk walk.

DIET:

Eat under 75 carbohydrates

DAY 6: SATURDAY

READING FOR REFLECTION

Nothing is so important to man as his own state, nothing is so formidable to him as eternity; and thus it is not natural that there should be men indifferent to the loss of their existence, and to the perils of everlasting suffering. They are quite different with regard to all other things. They are afraid of mere trifles; they foresee them; they feel them. And this same man who spends so many days and nights in rage and despair for the loss of office, or for some imaginary insult to his honour, is the very one who knows without anxiety and without emotion that he will lose all by death. It is a monstrous thing to see in the same heart and at the same time this sensibility to trifles and this strange insensibility to the greatest objects. It is an incomprehensible enchantment, and a supernatural slumber, which indicates as its cause an all-powerful force.

- Blaise Pascal, *Of the Necessity of the Wager*

DAY 6: SATURDAY

SPIRITUAL MEDIATION

(Find a quiet place to reflect. Breathe deeply and calm the mind. Once your heart rate slows, consider the following questions.)

α   Do I allow daily trifles to interrupt my goals?

α   Do I recognize that life is more than earthly honor and power? Or that death will ultimately find me and therefore my focus ought to be on lasting things?

α   Am I continuing to eat right in order to build my self-discipline?

DAY 7: SUNDAY

5:00 A.M. WAKE UP

40 push-ups
40 sit-ups
40 body squats

TODAY'S WORKOUT: CARDIO

Find a time today when you can devote 45
minutes to a brisk walk.

DIET:

Eat under 75 carbohydrates

DAY 7: SUNDAY

READING FOR REFLECTION

Beauty is not so much a fulfillment as rather a promise." In other words, by absorbing beauty with the right disposition, we experience, not gratification, satisfaction, and enjoyment but the arousal of an expectation; we are oriented toward something "not-yet-here". He who submits properly to the encounter with beauty will be given the sight and taste not of a fulfillment but of a promise--a promise that, in our bodily existence, can never be fulfilled. . . . Lovers and philosophers are connected by special ties, insofar as both erotic excitement and genuine philosophical quest trigger a momentum that, in this finite existence, can never be stilled. In an encounter with sensual beauty, if man opens up totally to the object of the encounter, a passion is born that, in the realm of the senses, which at first would seem to be the only adequate realm, can never be satisfied. The same holds true for the first moment of philosophical wonder (the wonder that arises from our contact with "reality"); a question arises that, in our finite world--which may mean, for example, with the tools of "science"--will also never receive an answer. The philosopher and the true lover-- neither will find fulfillment except through a divine favor.

— Josef Pieper, *Divine Madness: Plato's Case Against Secular Humanism*

DAY 7: SUNDAY

SPIRITUAL MEDIATION

(Find a quiet place to reflect. Breathe deeply and calm the mind. Once your heart rate slows, consider the following questions.)

α   What time in my life was I affected by beauty? An art piece, a song, a landscape, or another person?

α   How often do I allow myself time for authentic leisure? Not leisure from achieving my goals but time to re-fuel in order to be that much better at accomplishing them?

α   How is my body feeling today? Sore? Pumped? Rested? What can I do today to feel at my best?

DAY 8: MONDAY

5:00 A.M. WAKE UP

40 push-ups
40 sit-ups
40 body squats

TODAY'S WORKOUT: CHEST AND BACK

Incline Bench Press: 3 X 8
Flat Bench Dumbbell Press: 3 X 10
Incline Dumbbell Flyes: 3X 15
Dips: 3 sets to Failure

Deadlift: 3 X 6
Bent-over Barbell Rows: 3 X 8
Close-grip Cable Pulldowns: 3 x 10
Pull Ups: 3 sets to Failure

DIET:

Eat under 75 carbohydrates

DAY 8: MONDAY

READING FOR REFLECTION

The biggest adversary in our life is ourselves. We are what we are, in a sense, because of the dominating thoughts we allow to gather in our head. All concepts of self-improvement, all actions and paths we take, relate solely to our abstract image of ourselves. Life is limited only by how we really see ourselves and feel about our being. A great deal of pure self-knowledge and inner understanding allows us to lay an all-important foundation for the structure of our life from which we can perceive and take the right avenues.

— Bruce Lee

DAY 8: MONDAY

SPIRITUAL MEDIATION

(Find a quiet place to reflect. Breathe deeply and calm the mind. Once your heart rate slows, consider the following questions.)

α   Am I allowing my subjective doubts to get in the way of growing as a person?

α   How am I ridding myself of negative self-talk?

α   At the deepest part of who I am, what kind of person am I? Who do I want to be?

DAY 9: TUESDAY

5:00 A.M. WAKE UP

40 push-ups
40 sit-ups
40 body squats

TODAY'S WORKOUT: CARDIO

30 burpees
100 jumping jacks
20 burpees
15 minute jog on a treadmill or outside

DIET:

Eat under 75 carbohydrates

DAY 9: TUESDAY

READING FOR REFLECTION

It is not that we have a short space of time, but that we waste much of it. Life is long enough, and it has been given in sufficiently generous measure to allow the accomplishment of the very greatest things if the whole of it is well invested. But when it is squandered in luxury and carelessness, when it is devoted to no good end, forced at last by the ultimate necessity we perceive that it has passed away before we were aware that it was passing. So it is—the life we receive is not short, but we make it so, nor do we have any lack of it, but are wasteful of it. Just as great and princely wealth is scattered in a moment when it comes into the hands of a bad owner, while wealth however limited, if it is entrusted to a good guardian, increases by use, so our life is amply long for him who orders it properly.

— Seneca, *On the Shortness of Life*

DAY 9: TUESDAY

SPIRITUAL MEDIATION

(Find a quiet place to reflect. Breathe deeply and calm the mind. Once your heart rate slows, consider the following questions.)

α   How often do I look at my life to keep in check what is truly important?

α   What sacrifices can I make for someone else today?

α   In what ways am I prepared to keep moving forward in this journey of self-mastery?

DAY 10: WEDNESDAY

5:00 A.M. WAKE UP

40 push-ups
40 sit-ups
40 body squats

TODAY'S WORKOUT: LEGS AND SHOULDERS

Leg Press: 3 X 8
Squat: 3 X 8
Front Squat: 3 X 15
Weighted Lunges: 3 X 10

Seated front press: 3 X 8
Lateral dumbbell raises: 3 X 10
Front barbell raises: 3 X 10
Standing upright rows: 3 X 10

DIET:

Eat under 75 carbohydrates

DAY 10: WEDNESDAY

READING FOR REFLECTION

No matter how ruined man and his world may seem to be, and no matter how terrible man's despair may become, as long as he continues to be a man his very humanity continues to tell him that life has a meaning. That, indeed, is one reason why man tends to rebel against himself. If he could without effort see what the meaning of life is, and if he could fulfill his ultimate purpose without trouble, he would never question the fact that life is well worth living. Or if he saw at once that life had no purpose and no meaning, the question would never arise. In either case, man would not be capable of finding himself so much of a problem.

Our life, as individual persons and as members of a perplexed and struggling race, provokes us with the evidence that it must have meaning. Part of the meaning still escapes us. Yet our purpose in life is to discover this meaning, and live according to it. We have, therefore, something to live for. The process of living, of growing up, and becoming a person, is precisely the gradually increasing awareness of what that something is.

— Thomas Merton, *No Man is an Island*

DAY 10: WEDNESDAY

SPIRITUAL MEDIATION

(Find a quiet place to reflect. Breathe deeply and calm the mind. Once your heart rate slows, consider the following questions.)

α   What have the past ten days done in my life?

α   Am I fulfilling what it means to be a person by finding my purpose for living?

α   What physical challenge can I take on that I know will push me to excel?

DAY 11: THURSDAY

5:00 A.M. WAKE UP

50 push-ups
50 sit-ups
50 body squats

TODAY'S WORKOUT: CARDIO

10 X 30 Second Sprints with
60 seconds breaks between

DIET:

Eat under 75 carbohydrates

DAY 11: THURSDAY

READING FOR REFLECTION

The Saint is a medicine because he is an antidote. Indeed that is why the saint is often a martyr; he is mistaken for a poison because he is an antidote. He will generally be found restoring the world to sanity by exaggerating whatever the world neglects, which is by no means always the same element in every age. Yet each generation seeks its saint by instinct; and he is not what the people want, but rather what the people need. This is surely the very much mistaken meaning of those words to the first saints, "Ye are the salt of the earth," which caused the Ex-Kaiser to remark with all solemnity that his beefy Germans were the salt of the earth; meaning thereby merely that they were the earth's beefiest and therefore best. But salt seasons and preserves beef, not because it is like beef; but because it is very unlike it. Christ did not tell his apostles that they were only the excellent people, or the only excellent people, but that they were the exceptional people; the permanently incongruous and incompatible people; and the text about the salt of the earth is really as sharp and shrewd and tart as the taste of salt. It is because they were the exceptional people, that they must not lose their exceptional quality. "If salt lose its savour, wherewith shall it be salted?" is a much more pointed question than any mere lament over the price of the best beef. If the world grows too worldly, it can be rebuked by the Church; but if the Church grows too worldly, it cannot be adequately rebuked for worldliness by the world.

— G. K. Chesterton, *St. Thomas Aquinas*

DAY 11: THURSDAY

SPIRITUAL MEDIATION

(Find a quiet place to reflect. Breathe deeply and calm the mind. Once your heart rate slows, consider the following questions.)

α What flavor, salt, am I bringing into the world?

α What does my personal appearance say to others?

α How is my diet changing causing me to be more disciplined in the rest of my life?

DAY 12: FRIDAY

5:00 A.M. WAKE UP

50 push-ups
50 sit-ups
50 body squats

TODAY'S WORKOUT: LEGS AND SHOULDERS

Dumbbell Bicep Curls: 3 X 8
Barbell Inverted Curls: 3 X 10
Seated Preacher Curls: 3 X 12

French Press: 3 X 8
Rope Triceps Extensions: 3 X 10
Triceps Dips: 3 X 15

Pull-ups: 2 sets to failure

DIET:

Eat under 75 carbohydrates

DAY 12: FRIDAY

READING FOR REFLECTION

"The Barbarian hopes — and that is the mark of him, that he can have his cake and eat it too. He will consume what civilization has slowly produced after generations of selection and effort, but he will not be at pains to replace such goods, nor indeed has he a comprehension of the virtue that has brought them into being. Discipline seems to him irrational, on which account he is ever marveling that civilization, should have offended him with priests and soldiers.... In a word, the Barbarian is discoverable everywhere in this, that he cannot make: that he can befog and destroy but that he cannot sustain; and of every Barbarian in the decline or peril of every civilization exactly that has been true.

We sit by and watch the barbarian. We tolerate him in the long stretches of peace, we are not afraid. We are tickled by his irreverence; his comic inversion of our old certitudes and our fixed creed refreshes us; we laugh. But as we laugh we are watched by large and awful faces from beyond, and on these faces there are no smiles."
— Hilaire Belloc

DAY 12: FRIDAY

SPIRITUAL MEDIATION

(Find a quiet place to reflect. Breathe deeply and calm the mind. Once your heart rate slows, consider the following questions.)

α What disciplines am I shirking due to laziness or pride?

α What disciplines am I succeeding in?

α How has my view of others been? Do I look at character above all else or do I jump to conclusions before truly knowing the person?

DAY 13: SATURDAY

5:00 A.M. WAKE UP

50 push-ups
50 sit-ups
50 body squats

TODAY'S WORKOUT: CARDIO

Treadmill: 30 sec sprints uphill with 30 sec rest
between X 15

or Hills 15 sprints and walk back down

DIET:

Eat under 75 carbohydrates

DAY 13: SATURDAY

READING FOR REFLECTION

Remember, of these parents you were born; what can you give them for all they gave you?

With all your soul fear God and revere his priests.

With all your strength love your Maker and do not neglect his ministers.

Honor God and respect the priest; give him his portion as you have been commanded

First fruits and contributions, his portion of victims and holy offerings.

To the poor also extend your hand, that your blessing may be complete.

Give your gift to all the living, and do not withhold your kindness from the dead.

Do not avoid those who weep, but mourn with those who mourn.

Do not hesitate to visit the sick, because for such things you will be loved.

In whatever you do, remember your last days, and you will never sin.

— The Book of Sirach 7:28-36

DAY 13: SATURDAY

SPIRITUAL MEDIATION

(Find a quiet place to reflect. Breathe deeply and calm the mind. Once your heart rate slows, consider the following questions.)

α Do I consistently remember that one day I will die and live accordingly?

α How do I treat those who are suffering or in need?

α In what ways can I take the discipline I am earning and help my fellow man?

DAY 14: SUNDAY

5:00 A.M. WAKE UP

Read for 30 Minutes
Meditate for 5 Minutes
- Focus on your breathing and try to imagine you at your best

TODAY'S WORKOUT: STRETCH AND REST

DIET:

Eat under 75 carbohydrates

DAY 14: SUNDAY

READING FOR REFLECTION

"The repugnance to what must ensue almost immediately, and the uncertainty, were dreadful, he said; but worst of all was the idea, 'What should I do if I were not to die now? What if I were to return to life again? What an eternity of days, and all mine! How I should grudge and count up every minute of it, so as to waste not a single instant!' He said that this thought weighed so upon him and became such a terrible burden upon his brain that he could not bear it, and wished they would shoot him quickly and have done with it."

— Fyodor Dostoyevsky, *The Prince*

DAY 14: SUNDAY

SPIRITUAL MEDIATION

(Find a quiet place to reflect. Breathe deeply and calm the mind. Once your heart rate slows, consider the following questions.)

α   How would I live my life differently if I knew that I only had a month to live?

α   Can my life be expressed as a gift or a parasite to those around me?

α   How am I feeling? Are my muscles aching or growing? Is my mind exhausted or energized?

DAY 15: MONDAY

5:00 A.M. WAKE UP

60 push-ups
60 sit-ups
60 body squats

TODAY'S WORKOUT: CHEST AND BACK

Bench Press: 1 warm up set
                     2 sets to failure

Deadlift: 1 warm up set
                2 sets to failure

Wide Grip Pulldowns: 3 X 8
            Superset with:
Incline Dumbbell Press: 3 x 10

Push Ups: 3 sets to Failure

DIET:

Eat under 60 carbohydrates

DAY 15: MONDAY

READING FOR REFLECTION

Without food, the body quickly collapses; without spiritual food, the soul atrophies. It really is as simple as that. Though materialists of all stripes want to deny it, there is a dimension of the human person that goes beyond the merely physical, a dynamism that connects him or her with God. Classically, this link to the eternal is called the soul. (We oughtn't to construe this, by the way, in the Cartesian manner, as though the soul is imprisoned by the body. Rather, we ought to follow Thomas Aquinas who said, "the soul is in the body, not as contained by it, but containing it.")

What the soul requires for nourishment is the divine life or what the spiritual masters call "grace." It is of this sustenance that Jesus speaks in John 6: "Do not work for food that perishes but for the food that endures for eternal life." Most people are at least inchoately aware of the soul and its hunger, but they feed it with insufficient food: wealth, pleasure, power, and honor. All of these are good in themselves, but none of them is designed to satisfy the longing of the soul. And this is precisely why some of the wealthiest, most famous, and accomplished

people in our society are dying of spiritual
starvation.
— Bishop Robert Barron, *Why You Need Spiritual
Food*

DAY 15: MONDAY

SPIRITUAL MEDIATION

(Find a quiet place to reflect. Breathe deeply and
calm the mind. Once your heart rate slows,
consider the following questions.)

α Am I recognizing that inner hunger for
   more than what this world offers?

α How am I pushing my body to be more
   than just mediocre?

α What does Bishop Barron mean when he
   quotes Thomas Aquinas', "the soul is in
   the body, not as contained by it, but
   containing it."?

DAY 16: TUESDAY

5:00 A.M. WAKE UP

60 push-ups
60 sit-ups
60 body squats

TODAY'S WORKOUT: CARDIO

One hour long walk (Preferably after supper)

DIET:

Eat under 60 carbohydrates

DAY 16: TUESDAY

READING FOR REFLECTION

This then remains: Remember to retire into this little territory of thy own, and above all do not distract or strain thyself, but be free, and look at things as a man, as a human being, as a citizen, as a mortal. But among the things readiest to thy hand to which thou shalt turn, let there be these, which are two. One is that things do not touch the soul, for they are external and remain immovable; but our perturbations come only from the opinion which is within. The other is that all these things, which thou seest, change immediately and will no longer be; and constantly bear in mind how many of these changes thou hast already witnessed. The universe is transformation: life is opinion.

— Marcus Aurelius, *Meditations*

DAY 16: TUESDAY

SPIRITUAL MEDIATION

(Find a quiet place to reflect. Breathe deeply and calm the mind. Once your heart rate slows, consider the following questions.)

α Have I spoken negatively of myself in the past few days? Why? Was it irrational?

α What is my opinion of food? Is it fuel or just another chance to indulge?

α How do I react to others bad attitudes? With stoic reserve or quick negative reactions?

DAY 17: WEDNESDAY

5:00 A.M. WAKE UP

60 push-ups
60 sit-ups
60 body squats

TODAY'S WORKOUT: LEGS AND SHOULDERS

Squat: 1 warm up set
2 sets to failure

Standing Military Press: 1 warm up set
2 sets to failure

Seated Dumbbell Shoulder Flies: 3 X 8
Superset with
Walking Lunges: 3 sets 20 steps forward and back

DIET:

Eat under 60 carbohydrates

DAY 17: WEDNESDAY

READING FOR REFLECTION

In peace there's nothing so becomes a man
As modest stillness and humility:
But when the blast of war blows in our ears,
Then imitate the action of the tiger;
Stiffen the sinews, summon up the blood,
Disguise fair nature with hard-favour'd rage;
Then lend the eye a terrible aspect;
Let pry through the portage of the head
Like the brass cannon; let the brow o'erwhelm it
As fearfully as doth a galled rock
O'erhang and jutty his confounded base,
Swill'd with the wild and wasteful ocean.

— William Shakespeare, *Henry V*

DAY 17: WEDNESDAY

SPIRITUAL MEDIATION

(Find a quiet place to reflect. Breathe deeply and calm the mind. Once your heart rate slows, consider the following questions.)

α At what intensity do I live my life?

α Do I simply try and 'get by'?

α What areas are in me that I know need more attention in order to reach for perfection?

DAY 18: THURSDAY

5:00 A.M. WAKE UP

60 push-ups
60 sit-ups
60 body squats

TODAY'S WORKOUT: CARDIO

One hour long walk

DIET:

Eat under 60 carbohydrates

DAY 18: THURSDAY

READING FOR REFLECTION

I decline to accept the end of man. It is easy enough to say that man is immortal because he will endure: that when the last ding-dong of doom has clanged and faded from the last worthless rock hanging tideless in the last red and dying evening, that even then there will still be one more sound: that of his puny inexhaustible voice, still talking. I refuse to accept this. I believe that man will not merely endure: he will prevail. He is immortal, not because he alone among creatures has an inexhaustible voice, but because he has a soul, a spirit capable of compassion and sacrifice and endurance. The poet's, the writer's, duty is to write about these things. It is his privilege to help man endure by lifting his heart, by reminding him of the courage and honor and hope and pride and compassion and pity and sacrifice which have been the glory of his past. The poet's voice need not merely be the record of man, it can be one of the props, the pillars to help him endure and prevail.

- William Faulkner, *Nobel Prize Acceptance Speech*

DAY 18: THURSDAY

SPIRITUAL MEDIATION

(Find a quiet place to reflect. Breathe deeply and calm the mind. Once your heart rate slows, consider the following questions.)

α   How often do I bring hope, compassion, and honor into my conversations with others?

α   What 'immortal' legacy am I leaving?

α   Will I continue to push myself physically or have I decided to take the easy path?

DAY 19: FRIDAY

5:00 A.M. WAKE UP

60 push-ups
60 sit-ups
60 body squats

TODAY'S WORKOUT: ARMS

Barbell Curls: 1 warm up set
                 2 sets to failure

Close Grip Bench Press: 1 warm up set
                        2 sets to failure
Cable Rope Curls: 3 X 8
       Superset with
Cable Rope Triceps Extensions: 3 X 12

DIET:

Eat under 60 carbohydrates

DAY 19: FRIDAY

READING FOR REFLECTION

From the point of view of self-sufficiency the same result seems to follow; for the final good is thought to be self-sufficient. Now by self-sufficient we do not mean that which is sufficient for a man by himself, for one who lives a solitary life, but also for parents, children, wife, and in general for his friends and fellow citizens, since man is born for citizenship. But some limit must be set to this; for if we extend our requirement to ancestors and descendants and friends' friends we are in for an infinite series. Let us examine this question, however, on another occasion; the self-sufficient we now define as that which when isolated makes life desirable and lacking in nothing; and such we think happiness to be; and further we think it most desirable of all things, without being counted as one good thing among others- if it were so counted it would clearly be made more desirable by the addition of even the least of goods; for that which is added becomes an excess of goods, and of goods the greater is always more desirable. Happiness, then, is something final and self-sufficient, and is the end of action.

- Aristotle, *Ethics* Book 1

DAY 19: FRIDAY

SPIRITUAL MEDIATION

(Find a quiet place to reflect. Breathe deeply and calm the mind. Once your heart rate slows, consider the following questions.)

α How am I defining my happiness?

α Do I work towards self-sufficiency or do I purely rely on others for my necessities?

α What role are my material possessions playing in my life? Do they run me or do I own them?

DAY 20: SATURDAY

5:00 A.M. WAKE UP

60 push-ups
60 sit-ups
60 body squats

TODAY'S WORKOUT: CARDIO

Complete a total of 80 burpees

DIET:

Eat under 60 carbohydrates

DAY 20: SATURDAY

READING FOR REFLECTION

The battle, sir, is not to the strong alone; it is to the vigilant, the active, the brave. Besides, sir, we have no election. If we were base enough to desire it, it is now too late to retire from the contest. There is no retreat but in submission and slavery! Our chains are forged! Their clanking may be heard on the plains of Boston! The war is inevitable — and let it come! I repeat it, sir, let it come!

It is in vain, sir, to extenuate the matter. Gentlemen may cry, "Peace! Peace!" — but there is no peace. The war is actually begun! The next gale that sweeps from the north will bring to our ears the clash of resounding arms! Our brethren are already in the field! Why stand we here idle? What is it that gentlemen wish? What would they have? Is life so dear, or peace so sweet, as to be purchased at the price of chains and slavery? Forbid it, Almighty God! I know not what course others may take; but as for me, give me liberty, or give me death!

- Patrick Henry

DAY 20: SATURDAY

SPIRITUAL MEDIATION

(Find a quiet place to reflect. Breathe deeply and calm the mind. Once your heart rate slows, consider the following questions.)

α Am I winning my internal battles of overturning pride and negative self-talk?

α What battles have I won this week?

α Who in my life can I call to a similar life of self-discipline?

DAY 21: SUNDAY

5:00 A.M. WAKE UP

Read for 30 Minutes
Meditate for 5 Minutes
- Focus on your breathing and try to imagine you at your best

TODAY'S WORKOUT: STRETCH AND REST

DIET:

Eat under 50 carbohydrates

DAY 21: SUNDAY

READING FOR REFLECTION

Blessed are the poor in spirit: for theirs is the kingdom of heaven.

Blessed are they that mourn: for they shall be comforted.

Blessed are the meek: for they shall inherit the earth.

Blessed are they which do hunger and thirst after righteousness: for they shall be filled.

Blessed are the merciful: for they shall obtain mercy.

Blessed are the pure in heart: for they shall see God.

Blessed are the peacemakers: for they shall be called the children of God.

Blessed are they which are persecuted for righteousness' sake: for theirs is the kingdom of heaven.

— Jesus Christ, *Matthew Ch. 5. 3-10*

DAY 21: SUNDAY

SPIRITUAL MEDIATION

(Find a quiet place to reflect. Breathe deeply and calm the mind. Once your heart rate slows, consider the following questions.)

α   Do I consistently consider the other people in my relationships or do I lean towards selfishness?

α   Who can I comfort today?

α   In what ways can I use my physical nature to bring others peace of heart?

DAY 22: MONDAY

5:00 A.M. WAKE UP

75 push-ups
75 sit-ups
75 body squats

TODAY'S WORKOUT: CHEST AND BACK

Bench Press: 1 warm up set
              2 sets to failure (add 20 lbs. from
              last week's weight)

Deadlift: 1 warm up set
          2 sets to failure (add 20 lbs. from
          last week's weight)

Wide Grip Pulldowns: 3 X 8
          Superset with:
Incline Dumbbell Press: 3 x 10

Push Ups: 3 sets to Failure

DIET:

Eat under 50 carbohydrates

DAY 22: MONDAY

READING FOR REFLECTION

Whenever we take a purely psychological interest in ourselves and thus analyze our character in the manner of mere spectators, we peruse a false and sterile self-knowledge... The fact that the person in question happens to be ourselves merely intensifies our curiosity, without changing its quality. We experience ourselves as we would a character in a novel, without in any way feeling responsible for his defects.

This type of self-knowledge is not rooted in any willingness to change, and so it is completely sterile from the standpoint of moral progress. People who are wont to diagnose their blemishes in this neutral and purely psychological mood will draw from such discoveries no increased power to overcome their defects. On the contrary, such an indolently neutral self-knowledge will make them even more inclined to resign themselves to those defects as a matter of course. They are more remote from the chance of curing those ills than they would if they knew nothing about them. They are often disposed to admit their faults overtly, without restraint or reticence: not however from the motive of humility, nor under the impulse of guilt-consciousness, but because they pique themselves on presenting their vices, a psychologically absorbing sight.

- Dietrich Von Hildebrand,
  Transformation in Christ

DAY 22: MONDAY

SPIRITUAL MEDIATION

(Find a quiet place to reflect. Breathe deeply and calm the mind. Once your heart rate slows, consider the following questions.)

α Do I make excuses for my shortcomings by over analyzing myself psychologically?

α What sort of self-control am I hoping to gain?

α How has pushing myself physically helped me gain self-knowledge?

DAY 23: TUESDAY

5:00 A.M. WAKE UP

75 push-ups
75 sit-ups
75 body squats

TODAY'S WORKOUT: CARDIO

30 burpees
100 jumping jacks
20 burpees
15 minute jog on a treadmill or outside

DIET:

Eat under 50 carbohydrates

DAY 23: TUESDAY

READING FOR REFLECTION

"All that is gold does not glitter,

Not all those who wander are lost;

The old that is strong does not wither,

Deep roots are not reached by the frost.

From the ashes a fire shall be woken,

A light from the shadows shall spring;

Renewed shall be blade that was broken,

The crownless again shall be king."

— J.R.R. Tolkien, *The Fellowship of the Ring*

DAY 23: TUESDAY

SPIRITUAL MEDIATION

(Find a quiet place to reflect. Breathe deeply and calm the mind. Once your heart rate slows, consider the following questions.)

α In what do I place my hope?

α When is the last time I told my family that I love them?

α What root system am I building and nurturing?

DAY 24: WEDNESDAY

5:00 A.M. WAKE UP

75 push-ups
75 sit-ups
75 body squats

TODAY'S WORKOUT: LEGS AND SHOULDERS

Squat: 1 warm up set
   2 sets to failure (add 20 lbs. from last week's weight)

Standing Military Press: 1 warm up set
        2 sets to failure (add 20 lbs. from last week's weight)

Seated Dumbbell Shoulder Flies: 3 X 8
   Superset with
Walking Lunges: 3 sets 20 steps forward and back

DIET:

Eat under 50 carbohydrates

DAY 24: WEDNESDAY

READING FOR REFLECTION

"That only is true enlargement of mind which is the power of viewing many things at once as one whole, of referring them severally to their true place in the universal system, of understanding their respective values, and determining their mutual dependence. Thus is that form of Universal Knowledge . . . set up in the individual intellect, and constitutes its perfection."

— John Henry Newman, *The Idea of a University*, Discourse VI

DAY 24: WEDNESDAY

SPIRITUAL MEDIATION

(Find a quiet place to reflect. Breathe deeply and calm the mind. Once your heart rate slows, consider the following questions.)

α How seriously do I take my intellectual cultivation?

α How long has it been since I read an entire book?

α What book can I begin now?

DAY 25: THURSDAY

5:00 A.M. WAKE UP

75 push-ups
75 sit-ups
75 body squats

TODAY'S WORKOUT: CARDIO

One hour long walk

DIET:

Eat under 50 carbohydrates

DAY 25: THURSDAY

READING FOR REFLECTION

I have studied many times
The marble which was chiseled for me —
A boat with a furled sail at rest in a harbor.
In truth it pictures not my destination
But my life.
For love was offered me and I shrank from its
disillusionment;
Sorrow knocked at my door, but I was afraid;
Ambition called to me, but I dreaded the
chances.
Yet all the while I hungered for meaning in my
life.
And now I know that we must lift the sail
And catch the winds of destiny
Wherever they drive the boat.
To put meaning in one's life may end in
madness,
But life without meaning is the torture
Of restlessness and vague desire —
It is a boat longing for the sea and yet afraid.

-   Edgar Lee Masters, *George Gray*

DAY 25: THURSDAY

SPIRITUAL MEDIATION

(Find a quiet place to reflect. Breathe deeply and calm the mind. Once your heart rate slows, consider the following questions.)

α   What fears have I allowed in my life which are holding me back?

α   Which ambition of mine am I stifling?

α   What opportunity is available around me that I might be able to take advantage of?

DAY 26: FRIDAY

5:00 A.M. WAKE UP

75 push-ups
75 sit-ups
75 body squats

TODAY'S WORKOUT: ARMS

Barbell Curls: 1 warm up set
2 sets to failure (add 20 lbs. from last week's weight)

Close Grip Bench Press: 1 warm up set
2 sets to failure (add 20 lbs. from last week's weight)

Cable Rope Curls: 3 X 8
Superset with
Cable Rope Triceps Extensions: 3 X 12

DIET:

Eat under 50 carbohydrates

DAY 26: FRIDAY

READING FOR REFLECTION

Dear son, give thanks to God often for all the good things He has done for you, so that you may be worthy to receive more, in such a manner that if it please the Lord that you come to the burden and honor of governing the kingdom, you may be worthy to receive the sacred unction wherewith the kings of France are consecrated.

Dear son, if you come to the throne, strive to have that which befits a king, that is to say, that in justice and rectitude you hold yourself steadfast and loyal toward your subjects and your vassals, without turning either to the right or to the left, but always straight, whatever may happen. And if a poor man has a quarrel with a rich man, sustain the poor rather than the rich, until the truth is made clear, and when you know the truth, do justice to them.

If anyone have entered into a suit against you (for any injury or wrong which he may believe that you have done to him), be always for him and against yourself in the presence of your council, without showing that you think much of your case (until the truth be made known concerning it); for those of your council might be backward in speaking against you, and this you should not wish; and command your judges that you be not in any way upheld more than any others, for thus will your councilors judge more boldly according to right and truth.

- King St. Louis IX, *Letter to His Son*

DAY 26: FRIDAY

SPIRITUAL MEDIATION

(Find a quiet place to reflect. Breathe deeply and calm the mind. Once your heart rate slows, consider the following questions.)

α Am I humble enough to side with other before myself?

α Am I willing to stand up for truth though it may bring me pain?

α How can my lifting help me grow in humility?

DAY 27: SATURDAY

5:00 A.M. WAKE UP

75 push-ups
75 sit-ups
75 body squats

TODAY'S WORKOUT: CARDIO

Complete a total of 85 burpees

DIET:

Eat under 30 carbohydrates

DAY 27: SATURDAY

READING FOR REFLECTION

"A nation can survive its fools, and even the ambitious. But it cannot survive treason from within. An enemy at the gates is less formidable, for he is known and carries his banner openly. But the traitor moves amongst those within the gate freely, his sly whispers rustling through all the alleys, heard in the very halls of government itself. For the traitor appears not a traitor; he speaks in accents familiar to his victims, and he wears their face and their arguments, he appeals to the baseness that lies deep in the hearts of all men. He rots the soul of a nation, he works secretly and unknown in the night to undermine the pillars of the city, he infects the body politic so that it can no longer resist. A murderer is less to fear."

- Marcus Tullius Cicero

DAY 27: SATURDAY

SPIRITUAL MEDIATION

(Find a quiet place to reflect. Breathe deeply and calm the mind. Once your heart rate slows, consider the following questions.)

α   What internal enemies ought I eradicate from my life?

α   How am I living as a good citizen?

α   Do I vote according to right reason and give my political stance even though it might be unpopular?

DAY 28: SUNDAY

5:00 A.M. WAKE UP

100 push-ups
100 sit-ups
100 body squats

TODAY'S WORKOUT: STRETCH AND REST

DIET:

Eat under 30 carbohydrates

DAY 28: SUNDAY

READING FOR REFLECTION

"I am trying here to prevent anyone saying the really foolish thing that people often say about Him: I'm ready to accept Jesus as a great moral teacher, but I don't accept his claim to be God. That is the one thing we must not say. A man who was merely a man and said the sort of things Jesus said would not be a great moral teacher. He would either be a lunatic — on the level with the man who says he is a poached egg — or else he would be the Devil of Hell. You must make your choice. Either this man was, and is, the Son of God, or else a madman or something worse. You can shut him up for a fool, you can spit at him and kill him as a demon or you can fall at his feet and call him Lord and God, but let us not come with any patronizing nonsense about his being a great human teacher. He has not left that open to us. He did not intend to."

— C.S. Lewis, *Mere Christianity*

DAY 28: SUNDAY

SPIRITUAL MEDIATION

(Find a quiet place to reflect. Breathe deeply and calm the mind. Once your heart rate slows, consider the following questions.)

α   If others were to describe me honestly, what words would be used?

α   Have I made my decision on whether Jesus truly was and is God Incarnate or do I consistently consider just a moral teacher?

α   In the coming week, write one letter to a family member or a friend thanking them for who they are.

DAY 29: MONDAY

5:00 A.M. WAKE UP

100 push-ups
100 sit-ups
100 body squats

TODAY'S WORKOUT: FULL BODY

Dumbbell Swings (warm-ups) 3 – 15-20
- Upright Rowing – 3 x 8-12
- Bench Press – 3 x 8-12
- One-Arm Dumbbell Rows – 3 x 8-12
- Dumbbell Laterals/Flyes – 3 x 8-12
- Incline Press – 3 x 8-12
- Triceps Pushdown – 3 x 8-12
- Barbell Curls – 3 x 8-12
- Seated Dumbbell Curls – 3 x 8-12
- Regular Squats – 3 x 8-12 (superset with
- Light Barbell Pullovers – 3 x 8-12
- Breathing Squats – 1 x 20 (superset with
- Breathing Pullovers – 1 x 20
- Deadlifts – 2 x 8-12
- Good Mornings – 2 x 8-12

DIET:

Eat under 30 carbohydrates

DAY 29: MONDAY

READING FOR REFLECTION

An old man, going a lone highway,
Came, at the evening, cold and gray,
To a chasm, vast, and deep, and wide,
Through which was flowing a sullen tide.

The old man crossed in the twilight dim;
The sullen stream had no fear for him;
But he turned, when safe on the other side,
And built a bridge to span the tide.

"Old man," said a fellow pilgrim, near,
"You are wasting strength with building here;
Your journey will end with the ending day;
You never again will pass this way;
You've crossed the chasm, deep and wide-
Why build you this bridge at the evening tide?"

The builder lifted his old gray head:
"Good friend, in the path I have come," he said,
"There followeth after me today,
A youth, whose feet must pass this way.

This chasm, that has been naught to me,
To that fair-haired youth may a pitfall be.
He, too, must cross in the twilight dim;
Good friend, I am building this bridge for him."

-   Will Allen Dromgoole, The Bridge Builder

DAY 29: MONDAY

SPIRITUAL MEDIATION

(Find a quiet place to reflect. Breathe deeply and calm the mind. Once your heart rate slows, consider the following questions.)

α What will my legacy be?

α How am I defining my fate?

α In the coming days, invite someone to workout with you.

DAY 30: TUESDAY

5:00 A.M. WAKE UP

100 push-ups
100 sit-ups
100 body squats

TODAY'S WORKOUT: CARDIO

One hour long walk (Preferably after supper)

DIET:

Eat under 30 carbohydrates

DAY 30: TUESDAY

READING FOR REFLECTION

The intensity of your desire to acquire any special ability depends on character, on ambition.

Soldiers, all men in fact, are natural hero worshipers. Officers with a flare for command realize this and emphasize in their conduct, dress and deportment the qualities they seek to produce in their men. When I was a second lieutenant I had a captain who was very sloppy and usually late yet he got after the men for just those faults; he was a failure.

The troops I have commanded have always been well dressed, been smart saluters, been prompt and bold in action because I have personally set the example in these qualities. The influence one man can have on thousands is a never-ending source of wonder to me. You are always on parade. Officers who through laziness or a foolish desire to be popular fail to enforce discipline and the proper wearing of uniforms and equipment not in the presence of the enemy will also fail in battle, and if they fail in battle they are potential murderers. There is no such thing as: "A good field soldier:" you are either a good soldier or a bad soldier.

— General George S. Patton, *Letter to His Son*

DAY 30: TUESDAY

SPIRITUAL MEDIATION

(Find a quiet place to reflect. Breathe deeply and calm the mind. Once your heart rate slows, consider the following questions.)

α How will I allow the past 30 days to change me from here on out?

α What disciplines am I going to continue?

α Of the mind, body, and soul, which was most affected the past 30 days and how can I affect the others more?

CONGRATULATIONS!

YOU HAVE COMPLETED 30 DAYS OF OPTIMAL LIVING.

SUGGESTIONS FOR CELEBRATING:

Buy a bottle of Scotch or your favorite alcohol and enjoy a few drinks.

Buy a dessert and enjoy.

WHAT NOW?

You might also be asking, why did this stop on a Tuesday? There are a few reasons.

1. I want you to finish off the week on your own.
2. I want to shock you out of the monotony of relying on someone else.
3. I want you to succeed and you must do that on your own.

Now that you have completed the thirty days, you might be wondering what to do next. My suggestion is to continue on this journey. Find a good book, whether fiction or non-fiction and push yourself intellectually. Find a workout routine that works for you and stick with it for another 30 to 60 days. Keep asking yourself these quintessential questions about yourself, about your relationship to the divine and about your relationship with those around you.

If you struggle with enough discipline to continue without a guide, start the thirty days over!

LET ME KNOW WHAT YOU THOUGHT!

YOUR VICTORIES, YOUR STRUGGLES, ANYTHING AT ALL.

GO TO JAREDZIMMERER.COM AND CLICK THE CONTACT BUTTON

LET'S CONNECT

TWITTER: @JAREDZIMMERER

FACEBOOK: JAREDZIMMERERFITNESS

INSTAGRAM: JAREDZIMMERER

Made in the USA
Lexington, KY
14 September 2018